So Yo
How to Start a.. _ ___ ,
By C.C. North

Printed in the United States of America

First Printing, 2014

To C...thank you for believing. -C.C.

Table of Contents

Preface

So, you've decided you want to start an E-Boutique. Great! It's probably because you really love fashion and you have an eye for style. You're usually the woman other's look to for all the latest fashion and advice on what to wear. You're the girl who can forecast the newest trends and rock them all with ease and your own personal style. Or, you may have done your research and realized that U.S Consumers will spend $327 BILLION DOLLARS ONLINE by 2016 which is a 62% increase from $202 Billion Dollars in 2011. Whatever your reason is, I can help!

Starting an online business, or any business, can be very challenging. You often have the passion but lack the know-how. Sure, having an online boutique seems like a pretty simple business to foray into. In reality, it takes a lot of time, effort, and dedication to succeed. Being your own boss is one of the most challenging and rewarding accomplishments you will ever tackle. It is not for the easily discouraged or distracted.

Imagine living the life you want to live. Imagine your income matching your effort. Picture driving the car you love or finally taking that dream vacation. Wouldn't you love building a secure and stable future for yourself and those you love? This is all possible. Starting an E-Boutique will allow you to partake in a shift in how we all shop. 192 Million Americans will shop online by 2016. The time is now to act on a business that will allow you to make money while you sleep.

Once your E-Boutique is up and running, you are guaranteed to make money around the clock if you follow these 10 Steps I have detailed. These steps will include how to establish an E-Boutique, How to properly Social Network, E-Commerce Providers, How to Legally Establish Your Business the Right way, Choosing a Payment Processor, Finding Distributors, Attending Trade Shows, Obtaining Celebrity Endorsers, Email Marketing (How to Keep Your Loyal Customers Coming Back)

This guide is for Everyone! Beginners, those who have some knowledge of business, and those that want to learn proven tips of the trade to increase their income!

Learn how to increase your income and earn while you sleep by following the Steps in this guide!

Happy reading!

Remember: You will only and always receive what you work for.
Let's make it happen now!
-C.C. North

STEP ONE

How To Legally Establish Your E-Boutique

How to Obtain an EIN and Why

So at this point you've picked out your business name after much thought and consideration. I hope it is something that will stand the test of time and appeal to the customers you are trying to reach.

Now, you need to become a legal entity. This is necessary for a few very important reasons:

You need to have a business license and or EIN (Employee Identification number) in order to shop for your E-Boutique at trade shows and local and online wholesale distributors.

Also, establishing yourself legally will legitimize your business to your customers which will lay a foundation of trust. There are shoppers who are very much concerned with whom they spend their money with online. Even though online shopping is very convenient and opens a shopper's world up to a myriad of options, there is still a slight uneasiness that comes with sending money online to a business they may not be familiar with.

Now to get started, the first step after carefully selecting your business name, is to go online to www.IRS.gov and apply for an EIN (Employee Identification Number). The EIN will be issued immediately after correctly submitting your application. The application process is pretty straight forward and simple. The EIN is free of charge.

The purpose of getting an EIN for your E-Boutique is to establish your business legally with the IRS for tax purposes. Also, your EIN can be used to open a business bank account for your E-Boutique.

How to Obtain a Business License

Ok, now you have completed the first of many important steps. Congrats!

Your next step will be to obtain a business license in your City/State. The process varies by state. The most efficient way to find out your local business license procedures is to go to your state's .Gov site and search for "Applying for a Business License". As stated above, the process for obtaining a business license varies by state. Your State's .Gov site can give you more detailed information.

What's Next?

The next very important step to establishing your business legally is to register your business with your state's revenue office so you can legally collect sales tax on sales you make in the state.
To do so, simply go to your state's revenue office website or local office in person. Although this step can be completed online, if you need extra assistance, a visit to your local revenue office may be beneficial. At this point you will need your EIN (Employee Identification Number) to register your business with your state's revenue office.

The purpose of registering with your state's revenue is so that you can legally collect sales tax on all purchases made online that originate in the state where your business is registered. Meaning, if your business is registered in Ohio and you receive online sales from shoppers that live in Ohio, you must collect State Sales Tax on those sales and report those sales to your State Revenue Office. You will have to report and pay taxes on those sales. Sales taxes vary by state. Legally, this is very important and vital to your business.

BONUS TIP:
If you need help with having a logo designed for your E-Boutique, head over to www.Fiverr.com. You will find an endless selection of designers and the best part it only cost $5!

STEP TWO

Finding Distributors

Now, this is one of the most exciting and fun parts. Obviously you love shopping and this is where you get to flex your fashion acumen. To start, the best place to find distributors is locally. Search out your local fashion wholesale markets. Luckily, this can be accomplished with a simple Google search. For those of you who live in smaller towns and don't have access to local wholesale distributors, the next option would be to see if there are any local trade shows where fashion distributors gather together and introduce their new products to business owners like yourself. You can find this information by doing a Google search for Fashion Trade shows in your area.

Beyond locally, there are literally thousands of online wholesale distributors. This is where having your EIN, Business License, and State Sales Tax License come in handy. Most online wholesalers require this information from your business before you can view their complete product line and pricing.

Finding distributors locally and online is a good way for the beginner E-Boutique owner to shop for inventory for their E-Boutique. Shopping locally will allow you to learn how to deal with wholesalers. Remember they are business owners as well and understand what you are trying to accomplish. They are usually a good source of help when you are starting out. Remember to always be kind to your local wholesalers. A good tip is to develop a relationship with the sales people. They do remember customers who spend well and shop often but they also remember the person with the great attitude who doesn't always try to lowball their prices.

What to Expect at the Wholesale Markets?

You will have to register your business with the Wholesale store so make sure to bring your EIN, Business License, and State Sales Tax License. Always have a copy of these on you when you are shopping for your E-Boutique. They are a requirement at any reputable distributor. You only have to register once, and you're set to shop 'til you drop!

Most local wholesale markets receive new inventory 2-3 times a week. Talk to the sales people to find out when these days are. Another option is to be added to their email list or see if the store has a website that list their new products. Once again, this is where developing a good relationship with the sales people in the stores come into play. Once you have an inside man or woman, they will most likely call or text you with new arrivals before anyone else receives them. This will definitely give you an advantage. You definitely want to be the E-Boutique with the most exclusive items. Even if you do carry popular widespread items, it does help if you have them before anyone else. This is definitely the reputation you want to build for your E-Boutique.

STEP THREE

Quick Guide to Attending Trade Shows

Major Trade Shows-Magic

Every February and August a major fashion trade show is held in wonderful Las Vegas called Magic. You can pre-register for this event online (http://www.magiconline.com/register-now). This event is major in every sense of the word! Magic showcases fashion vendors from around the world. This is where you need to be if you want to take your business to the next level. This is where all of the upcoming season's hottest fashions will be showcased. Magic is where you can and will make amazing connections for the advancement of your E-Boutique.

Shopping locally is just fine, and you can absolutely operate your E-Boutique while shopping at your local wholesale markets. They may just be that great. Especially if you live in or near Los Angeles, CA, USA which is the wholesale market mecca and has hundreds of wholesale stores to shop at locally and online. But, if you want to try something a bit different and connect with a broader range of distributors, large and small, Magic in Las Vegas (Every February and August) may definitely be worth checking out for your E-Boutique.

Now, when you go to Las Vegas for Magic, have a budget for your store and also if you have the time make your way to Los Angeles. It is a 1-hour flight or a 3-and-a-half-hour drive and totally worth it. As you may know, you may only select your clothing at the shows and then they will be mailed to you. Well, if you have the time and if they are ready, you can simply head to LA, pick them up, peruse and shop more stores, and take some of your inventory home with you. I think it is a great opportunity to take advantage of being in close proximity to two shopping meccas. Seize it!

Smaller Trade Shows

Now, if you live in a major city such as Los Angeles, Dallas, New York or Atlanta count yourself lucky. Each of these cities either have their own local trade shows or a major wholesale shopping district. If you do not live in one of these cities, no problem. You may not be able to see products in person immediately but some of these places allow you to shop online. Google the city you are most interested in along with wholesale products you are searching for your E-Boutique. Your search should look something like below:

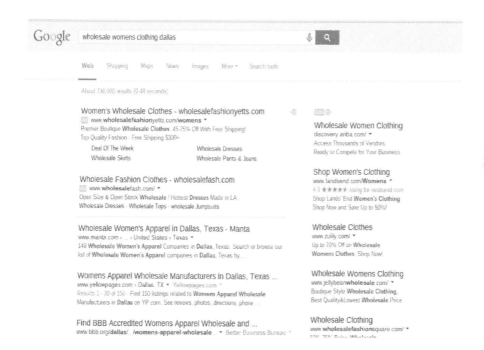

Now, you can apply this same search to any of the major cities or even the city you reside in. Just because you do not like in a major city does not mean there are not wholesale stores or trade shows available for you to attend for your E-Boutique. Google is your friend! The reason why I will not list wholesale stores individually is because every person's style is different. Every E-Boutique owner has a different vision for their store. E-Boutique Owner A may be targeting young party girl shoppers and E-Boutique Owner B may be targeting the more mature shopper. Make sure you search out wholesale stores that are specific to your E-Boutique's style needs.

Once you find and select online wholesale stores that is only the beginning. The next important step is to search out your local trade shows. As I stated above, Google is your friend. Here is a sample search for trade shows in New York:

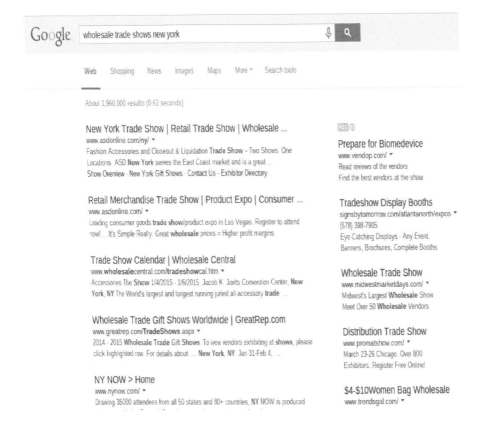

Ok, not everyone lives in New York. Simply tailor this search to the city you live in. If the city you live in does not have many or any trade shows, look up the nearest major city.

Never give up when you are searching or in business period. Your persistence will pay off. If being an E-Boutique business owner was easy, everyone would do it. Even if they try, only the hardworking and tenacious will succeed. Most small businesses fail within the first 3 years. On the flip side, your E-Boutique can excel exceedingly well with a tough, determined boss such as yourself. You have taken the most important step by purchasing this book as a guide to success.

"Today knowledge has power. It controls access to opportunity and advancement" - Peter Drucker

At your fingertips you have complete access to success. You need to find new wholesalers to supply inventory because you might be experiencing problems with the current vendors you do business with? Search them out. Google is your friend. Looking for new styles or new companies to work with? Google is your friend. You can never hit a brick wall. Always push through until you are satisfied with the results. This is vital to the success of your E-Boutique.

Before you arrive at the trade shows, make sure to check out the vendors that will be there if this information is available (it usually is). I encourage you to check out as many vendors as possible, but it is always good to have a game plan before you arrive. Map out and visit the vendors you are most interested in. Then make your way around to the other vendors. Doing your research before you arrive will save you a lot of time and keep you focused while you are there.

After you have searched for trade shows and selected the ones you would like to attend, the next step is to register. Most tradeshows require you to register before you arrive. You will most likely need to fax or email your EIN, Business License, State Sales Tax License and invoices from previous purchase from other wholesalers for your E-Boutique. This is a simple and straightforward process. Once you have registered, they will either mail you your badge to attend the event or have it ready for you to pick up once you arrive.

Now, have fun and happy shopping! You are on your way to success!

BONUS: To Shop Alibaba/AliExpress or not?

If you are not familiar with Alibaba or AliExpress I will give you a quick lesson:

Alibaba is an online sourcing platform based in China. Meaning, if you are a designer and want your designs mass produced or see a design that you want mass produced, you can upload your design and have manufacturers in China bid for your business.

AliExpress is an online wholesale market based in China. You can go on AliExpress and buy everything from clothing, hair, jewelry and electronics. Prices are based on quantity purchased which works in the favor of those who buy in bulk quantities such as E-Boutique owners like yourself.

The good thing about both of these websites are the low prices and unlike American wholesalers, business credentials are not required. It is an open market for anyone who wants to purchase online.

The not so good thing is that most of the sellers and manufacturers are based in China. That means long turnaround times, package delays at customs, unscrupulous sellers, and ill-fitting products. Now, this is not the case for every single seller that sells products on these websites. These are only a representation of certain situations that may occur when dealing with any overseas purchase.

My advice is to read reviews. The good and bad reviews are important to read because a bad review may not always mean a bad product. It could simply be a slight shipping delay that was resolved. Alternatively, a good review could mean that the product was received but was ill fitting. Both of these are important and can determine whether or not the seller should get your business.

Doing your research is important when dealing with any wholesaler. Taking a few extra minutes to do your research can save you lots of money, disappointment, and time.

The good thing about shopping at AliExpress is the variety of clothing. They definitely have a myriad of cool and unique clothing that an E-Boutique owner looking for exclusive items would love.

Keep in mind that sizing in Asia is very different from US sizing. A lot of the items are sold in a size called Free Size. Free Size will probably fit up to a US Size Medium. When the clothing is not Free Size and have actual sizes, the seller on AliExpress will usually include a size chart. Please pay close attention to the measurements on the size chart. AliExpress size charts are usually listed in centimeters and not inches which makes a huge difference. Here is an example of a size chart from AliExpress:

www.aliexpress.com/item/New-Brand-2014-Sexy-Womens-Clubwear-Dress-Black-Mesh-Panel-Knee-Length-Mini-Dress-High-Waist/1907017...

| Product Details | Feedback (535) | Shipping & Payment | Seller Guarantees |

body measurement really matches to this set. All measurement is in cm and please note 1cm=0.39inch)

· Weight :200g (approx.)

ITEM SIZE

SIZE CHART

Size			Bust	Waist	Hip	Length
US	AU/UK	EURO	CM	CM	CM	CM
S	2	6	32	76cm	54cm	78cm	95cm
	4	8	34	90cm	66cm	90cm	
M	6	10	36	78cm	62cm	84cm	99cm
	8	12	38	92cm	70cm	94cm	
L	10	14	40	80cm	64cm	86cm	101cm
	12	16	42	94cm	72cm	96cm	
XL	14	18	44	86cm	68cm	92cm	103cm
	16	20	46	96cm	82cm	100cm	
XXL	18	22	48	88cm	76cm	94cm	108cm
	20	24	50	98cm	86cm	102cm	

Notice the measurements? They are very different in comparison to US sizes. They are listed in centimeters and not inches which makes a huge difference in sizing. Note the differences when you are selecting and buying for your E-Boutique. Paying close attention to detail in all aspects of business will be of great benefit to you. Especially when you are purchasing inventory from Asia and abroad.

This is my honest and unbiased opinion about these websites and shopping from them as an E-Boutique owner.

STEP FOUR

Finding an E-Commerce Provider

Wow! Look at all the progress you have made! You've legally established your business and picked out clothing for your E-Boutique that you just know that your target customers are going to LOVE. Now, it is time to make another very important step. It is time to buy the domain for your E-Boutique and select and E-Commerce Provider.

Buying the domain for your business further legitimizes your business. Whatever platform you choose as your E-Commerce provider will provide you with a domain extension name such as e.g www.EBoutique123.ECommProvider.com but, it looks a lot more professional to buy your domain and have your E-Boutique listed as www.EBoutique123.com .

There are plenty of places to buy your domain name but one of the most popular is www.GoDaddy.com. I love them personally, because of their prices and efficient service. You can do a quick search to see if your business name is available as an online domain and if it is you may purchase your domain name and other services from there. If your domain name is not available, don't fret. Try changing the spelling until you find an available domain or choose from one of the suggested domain names provided by GoDaddy.

If you do not want to change the spelling or alternate the spelling of your business name, they may offer you a .net instead of a .com. There may be alternate extensions available and if they are, they will be offered at that time.

While checking out, GoDaddy will list available products for you to purchase. These are totally optional but one that is definitely worth checking out and purchasing is a personal email for your business. Your customers will definitely feel more comfortable spending their hard earned money with a business that has its own email e.g CustomerCare@EBoutique123.com as opposed to Eboutique123CustomerCare@Yahoo.com. These small details matter in legitimizing and looking professional to customers who are already wary about online shopping.

Another option is Google domains. I love them equally. The setup is super quick and user friendly. They offer the same options as GoDaddy and their prices are affordable. I also like that they will let you incorporate your existing Google email address into your domain address. They do this by letting you create an email address that uses your newly created domain name, but the new emails go straight to your existing email so no extra email boxes which cuts down clutter. So simple! There are many places to buy your domain name, but I am directing you to the most user friendly and affordable options.

Quick tip: What I also love about buying my domain from Google domains and setting up my email through them is getting work emails directly to my phone. I always have my phone with me so I can check my work emails wherever I am with the Gmail app. Whether I'm at lunch, on vacay, I can check my emails and get back to what I'm doing, so simple!

Once you buy your domain name, your next step is to select an E-Commerce provider. There is a wide range of E-Commerce providers in terms of pricing and beneficial services that they offer to you as an E-Boutique owner.

If you are just starting out and are price conscious, a good option for your E-Boutique will definitely be www.BigCartel.com. Big Cartel is pro small business owner. Their pricing is based on the number of items your store carries. Their pricing plans allow you to list at 5 products for Free and up to 300 products for $29.99. You can fully customize your store and track inventory automatically. They allow you to easily transfer and use your own domain. You'll also be able to track visitors to your store, create discount codes and add up to 5 images per product. The setup is super easy, even for beginners! If you have no experience designing an online store, they have about 5 ready to use themes with easily customizable options such as the color of your font and the font type.

As I stated earlier there are plenty of E-Commerce providers but in my own personal experience Big Cartel is by far the easiest and quickest to set up for beginner E-Boutique owners. Their pricing for what they offer cannot be beat.

My next choice based on ease of setup and the help they offer only would be Shopify. I have used them, and I love everything that they have to offer. They are outstanding at integrating every feature that is needed to help you succeed at business. The only catch is that they are expensive if you are starting out. I only mention them because I highly recommend that you switch to them as soon as you can afford them because they are worth it. The analytics, the abandoned cart reports, product reviews, seo…etc the list goes on, but Shopify is worth it. They are a great company that truly cares about entrepreneurs.

STEP FIVE

Choosing a Payment Processor

Choosing a payment processor is a fairly easy decision based on which E-Commerce platform you decide to use for your E-Boutique. If you decide to go with my suggestion of Big Cartel, your payment processor will be PayPal or Stripe. PayPal is one of the biggest and widely trusted Payment Processors available to E-Boutique owners. Stripe is a fairly new payment processor. They are new but, trustworthy and easy to setup. They also allow your customers to checkout directly on your site unlike PayPal which redirects them to their site to checkout. The only drawback to Stripe is you have to wait 1-2 business days to receive payments. They send them to your bank account. They do not offer debit cards like PayPal.

PayPal is also one of the most widely used payment processors on E-Commerce platforms. You will most likely have PayPal as an option no matter which E-Commerce platform you select.

Whether or not you choose to use your E-Commerce platform built in payment processor, it is always a good idea to set up and establish a PayPal Business Account. One in 4 consumers will pay using PayPal online, when it is an available option. You will need your EIN (Employee Identification Number) to set up your PayPal Business Account. The process to set up your E-Boutique PayPal Business Account is fairly simple and quick. All of this can be done online directly on www.Paypal.com.

PayPal and other Payment Processors do charge a very small percentage of every transaction processed through them. This is common and the cost of doing business online. Opening an online business is a very cost-efficient way to becoming an entrepreneur and business owner but you have to take into account these small cost because they do add up. They will not break your bank, even as they add up over time, but as a business owner it is important to account for every dollar you spend to determine your bottom line.

STEP SIX

How to Properly Use Social Networks

In this day and age, everyone uses the internet. I know 8-year old children and grandparents with Facebook pages which is an indication of how vast internet usage is currently. As a business, it is very important to the success of your business that you have an online presence on Social Networks.

Why is Social networking so important? Social networking will be very vital to the success of your business. There are not many platforms like Facebook, Twitter, Instagram, Pinterest, etc.… With these social networks you will be able to tap into unlimited potential shoppers. Shoppers that you may never have connected with, for FREE I must add, online or offline.

As soon as your E-Boutique is up and running the very next step should be to create business accounts on the social networks you know how to use efficiently and have a clear understanding of how to work them. It is important to your E-Boutique to build an organic following on the social networks you choose.

The big Three of Social Networking for me personally is Facebook, Twitter and Instagram in no particular order. Facebook and Twitter offer paid advertising for businesses that allow you to pay for more promotion of your tweets and post. Is it worth it? If you build an organic following, paying to promote tweets or post may give you a return on your investment and it may not. Shoppers are smart and while some may not mind the promoted content, some may view it as spam and totally ignore your promoted post. Bottom line, it is worth a try. At the very least you will reach a wider audience with promoted post and/or tweets. Should you decide to give it a try your promoted content should include a Sale or offer specific to Facebook or Twitter. That way you will know exactly where your sales are coming from and if the paid promotion is worth it.

As I stated, you can still use Facebook and Twitter for Free without paying for anything at all. The reason for the promoted post is that even though a shopper may follow your E-Boutique Facebook page your post may not show up in their news feed unless they specifically select to follow your feed. This is Facebook's way of getting your advertising dollars. Promoted post are just an option if you want to gain more exposure.

My favorite of the three is Instagram. Instagram is guaranteed to show your post to everyone who follows you unlike Facebook, hence the promoted post. Instagram also allows you to follow up to 7500 people at a time. Now, what if these people do not follow you back? That's no good because you only want to follow users who engage actively in your E-Boutique Instagram post. A great way to weed out those who do not follow or engage in the content you post is to download an app(in your App Store or Google Play) that allows you to see your "Ghost" followers(users who do not engage in the content you post or who do not follow you back). Some of the apps are free and some run .99 and up. These apps are very useful and worth every penny. You should always keep an eye on who you're following because every single one of those followers is a potential shopper. It is also important that you realize that social networking is a two-way street. It is very nice to get lots of likes and comments, but it is very important that you engage with your followers and like and comment on their post as well.

Posting on these social networks should be a part of your daily routine. Your post should of course include all of the wonderful items from your E-Boutique. You should also include other content to keep your shoppers engaged. We'll call this the "filler". Be sure to include some of your favorite quotes, beautiful pics and whatever else that you may have a particular interest in that you would like to share. Always make sure that the content that you post is politically correct (no crazy space cadet views) and basically "happy" (have them associate funny and happy with your E-Boutique). Imagine your social networks as an online community that you are creating with beautiful clothing, kind words, funny quotes, and cool pics. Leave the crazy stuff to the 9'o clock news.

I will say it once again; you must make time to post consistently on your social networks. I don't think most new business owners realize the power and earning potential behind social networking. It can totally break or make your E-Boutique into a million-dollar business. We have word of mouth marketing where a satisfied customer may tell 2-3 friends about your business and then we have the online word of mouth where customers can spread positive reviews to millions of people in seconds. Use this (mostly) free advertising to your advantage and as often as you can. You should post at least 3 times a day on your social networks. It is better for customers to get tired of you posting than them to wonder where you are. Most customers will not hunt you down to find out where are your new products. They will simply find another E-Boutique to purchase from. That is definitely not what any business owner wants.

Also, remember the Golden Rule: Treat others how you want to be treated. Be nice to those you interact with on your social networks for your E-Boutique. There are people who spend their days harassing others on the internet and you must not stoop to their level. A customer will see your bad reaction and view that as a representation of you and your E-Boutique which is not good for business at all. Always remember that everyone watching is a potential shopper. Having a great attitude at all times when conducting business does matter and is very important to you having a one-time sale or loyal customer.

To sum this up in steps:

1. Instagram is completely free and will show your content to everyone who follows you.

2. Facebook and Twitter allow you to post for free but also offer promoted post and tweets.

3. Post at least 3 times a day on your social networks to keep your users engaged. Post "filler" content of things that are pertinent to your E-Boutique.

4. Download an app for Instagram that allows you to track your "Ghost" follower's i.e. Followers who do not engage in the content you post. This will allow you to weed out people that are not interested in the content you post.

5.	Post quality pics of clothing from your E-Boutique. If you do not have a model and use mannequins for your clothing, purchase an in home studio if you have the space, from Amazon.com or Ebay.com They have them for sale for under $100. You can also buy a nice camera for around the same price at Amazon.com or Ebay.com. It won't be a professional photographer's camera but, it will definitely get the job done well.

6.	Now who to follow? Search hashtags on Instagram for your target shopper. Is it the single girl with a great job that allows her to travel a lot? Search for fun hashtags such as #GirlsNightOut or #SexandtheCity, and hot travel destinations such as #StBarths or #Bali. Things and places a single woman with no responsibilities that has extra income (to shop with you!) might do more or more likely to travel to. You have to get into the minds of your shoppers. I call this "Targeting". "Targeting" will allow you to keep your Instagram followers full of potential shoppers. Always keep in mind your target shopper when you are looking for people to follow on Instagram. This equals a quality follower list and ultimately more $$$$$$ for you!

7.	As much time that you spend on selecting and buying inventory for your E-Boutique should be spent on you building your business' online presence on the social networks that you choose to use. Social networking will definitely contribute to the success of your business if used properly. Follow these 7 steps and make money while you sleep.

STEP SEVEN

How to Get a Celebrity to Endorse Your E-Boutique!

Another efficient way to market your E-Boutique is to have a celebrity endorse your clothing on all of their social networks. At this point it is worth noting that you should realize that marketing is the name of the game. Imagine you gaining 5,000-10,000 followers and potential customers all organically? Just because one of your favorite celebrity's wore something from your E-Boutique! Picture the instant boost in followers (potential shoppers) and sales.

This is all possible. We all start from somewhere and no one knows this better than your favorite celebrity. Not only do some celebs welcome the opportunity to help but they love FREE stuff just like the rest of us. I will teach you how to gain celebrity endorsers for your E-Boutique in just a few simple steps.

Start by identifying a few of your favorite celebrities that you feel embodies the essence of your E-Boutique. Is it your favorite reality star who you can totally relate to as you watch her storyline unfold week after week? Is it one of your favorite singers? As long as you know you target customer can relate to your celebrity endorsers and it is someone they can connect with on some level.

After you have identified these celebrity endorsers it's time to get their attention! Follow their Facebook page, Twitter feed, and Instagram page and actively engage with them.

Once you have gotten their attention it is time to search out their contact information. Depending on the celebrity you may be able to contact them directly through email. If it is a larger celebrity, they may only have contact for their management. It is also a good idea to follow their management if they have social network pages as well. Contact them respectfully and professionally and let them know all about your E-Boutique and that you would love to send them (your favorite celebrity) some items from your E-Boutique. Some celebrity's and/or their management respond right away and some never respond at all. It is always another celebrity endorser out there for you. Do not give up if you are rejected and have some other celebrity endorsers in mind in case you are rejected. You may get a few ignored/unanswered emails or flat out denials before you land a celebrity endorser but, it is definitely worth the effort.

Once you have secured your first celebrity endorser make sure you send them at least 3 items from your E-Boutique in the correct sizes expeditiously in the mail. It is important to treat your celebrity endorsers just as you would a customer. You are building a mutually beneficial relationship with them that you want to last. The right celebrity endorser may help you grow your E-Boutique business by leaps and bounds overnight. Make sure you choose wisely.

STEP EIGHT

Email Marketing

At this point you are building up your social network, gaining followers and shoppers. The most important thing is keeping them shopping with you. Here is how to accomplish repeat sales!

One of the most tried and true ways of maintaining customer relationships and loyalty is through email marketing. Email marketing is a guaranteed way to maintain customer loyalty. Every time a customer makes a purchase, they should provide you with an email. With their permission you may add their email address to your email marketing list. One of the best email marketing services for E-Boutiques is www.MailChimp.com. I love MailChimp because of the ease of use for beginners. Their prices are very reasonable for small business owners. You will pay only $15 per month to send unlimited marketing emails for up to 500 emails. They have a great and easy to use email design center for beginners and advanced users alike.

I love how simple and effective email marketing is. Here is why:

With a couple of clicks you'll be able to alert everyone who has purchased from your E-Boutique of all of your New Arrivals, Latest Sales, and Upcoming Events. This is a great way to gain repeat shoppers. Email marketing is also great because it gives your loyal shoppers the option to share all of the great deals they receive from your E-Boutique with their family and friends if you decide to include that option.

Email marketing is a sure way to maintain a constant presence with your loyal shoppers. You definitely want to create deals and sales for email subscribers to create a sense of exclusivity. Marketing to your loyal shoppers through email is also a great way to stay at the forefront of their shopping mind.

Ex. Loyal Shopper A is looking for a date night outfit. They just received a 20% off or Free Shipping marketing email from you on Monday evening. They know that if they order Monday night they can use the coupon you sent in their favorite E-Boutique (that's you) marketing email and have their date night outfit before the weekend.

Timing is very important when marketing your E-Boutique by e-mail. Put yourself in your shopper's shoes. When are you most likely to check your personal email? Is it usually after you get home and finally get a chance to unwind? What time is that? 7pm? 8pm? Now think about your customers. Most of them are not that much different from you. Peak time to send your marketing email and it actually get read is between 6pm-12am. This is when people are finally settled in at home after work and can catch a breather and get time to check their email and do some online shopping. If you send an email at 2pm when your shopper is at work, they may get a chance to view your email but put it on the backburner. They'll say "Great deal! I'll check it out once I get home" and most never do or forget. So, it's very important to send your marketing emails during peak hours of 6pm-12am.

MailChimp allows you to track opens and clickthrough's. Clickthrough's are shoppers who actually open your marketing email and click on a link to your website. Clickthrough's are as good as money! You want your email to be compelling enough for your shopper to want to view your E-Boutique and shop away.

Important things to consider are color themes. Were you aware that there is a psychology behind colors and shopping? Think of a few major businesses that you frequent. Most restaurants use red and yellow because yellow inspires happiness and friendliness while red stimulates your appetite and hunger. Combined they create a sense of urgency and feeling of needing to hurry up, eat and leave.

When selecting a color scheme for your E-Boutique business logo and marketing emails be sure to pick colors that are representative of what you are trying to convey to you shoppers. Use the provided color graph to help you select the colors that embodies the message you are trying to send to your shoppers.

BLACK
sophistication
power
mystery
formality
evil
death

GRAY
stability
security
strength of character
authority
maturity

PURPLE
royalty
luxury
dignity
wisdom
spirituality
passion
vision
magic

YELLOW
joy
cheerfulness
friendliness
intellect
energy
warmth
caution
cowardice

WHITE
freshness
hope
goodness
light
purity
cleanliness
simplicity
coolness

PINK
romance
compassion
faithfulness
beauty
love
friendship
sensitivity

RED
danger
passion
daring
romance
style
excitement
urgency
energetic

BLUE
peace
stability
calmness
confidence
tranquility
sincerity
affection
integrity

GREEN
life
growth
environment
healing
money
safety
relaxation
freshness

Use these simple tips to help you turn one-time sales into loyal shoppers. Create an email that is worth clicking through to your E-Boutique. Send your shoppers an email that they immediately want to share with their family and friends! Share emails that include only your best deals. Create a community of exclusivity that lets those subscribed to your email list know that they are absolutely receiving the best deals and newest products.

Email marketing will help your business maintain its loyal shoppers and create customer loyalty. It is proven that it is easier to maintain loyal shoppers then it is to acquire new shoppers. Treat your loyal shoppers with the utmost care. Remember that you are successful because of them.

STEP NINE

Choosing a Shipping Provider

Choosing a shipping provider for your E-Boutique may seem like a small easy task. You're probably thinking you want the fastest and cheapest shipping option. Fast and cheap works out for you and your shoppers. We all know that fast and cheap isn't always the best idea but in this instance it is. Shipping providers will literally chase you down for your business. Here is why:

They know that some of their best customers are small businesses like your E-Boutique.

Companies do not often switch shipping providers. Why? There is a big monopoly on shipping. There are literally a handful of providers that you can choose from. It is best to choose your shipping provider based on the specific needs for your E-Boutique.

The most popular with the lowest prices is the United States Postal Service. Other popular shipping options are UPS and FedEx. Guess who is the U.S. Post Office's biggest customers? UPS and FedEx are. How does that work out? Well, there are packages that are sent through UPS and FedEx that are delivered to your local U.S. Post Office who in turn deliver them to the customer. So, you might as well save money and utilize the U.S. Post Office's great flat rate shipping options and speedy services.

Once you have selected your shipping provider for your E-Boutique the next step is to acquire proper shipping materials. Remember you have to represent professionalism in your business from start to finish. The sale is not over once you have their money, it is the beginning. You want to make every customer a repeat customer and that begins when they receive their purchase in a nice package in a timely manner through your shipping provider.

How to Properly Pack Orders

Please do not ball up your shopper's purchase and ship it off. Shoppers shop at your E-Boutique for that exclusive, indie, authentic feel. Do not lose a customer by being careless with the packaging of their purchase. This will be their first impression of the service you provide along with the wonderful clothing they will receive from your E-Boutique.

Example of great packaging:

Do not be apprehensive about trying something other than your shipping providers envelopes or packaging. It is ok to step out of the box and try something different as far as shipping materials.

If at all possible, always attach printed shipping labels to your package. If you have a printer this can be accomplished at home.

Here is an example of printed shipping labels:

These labels can be purchased at your local Wal-Mart or any office supply store. Shop around for great deals on www.Amazon.com or www.Ebay.com if you will be purchasing these shipping labels in bulk.

After you have found the best deal on your shipping labels, the next step is to select your packaging. Now remember, you can always go to your shipping provider's physical location and pick up free packaging and shipping labels. You will have to hand print your customer's information which is not as professional as having the uniformity of printed labels. But, if you would like to choose your own packaging and if it is an option with your shipping provider(some only allow you to use their packaging), a great option is poly packaging.

Here is an example of poly packages:

These bags can be a great option because of the versatility in the sizing and colors. They are also very affordable which is always a plus. They can be purchased online at www.Amazon.com or www.Ebay.com.

The most important thing is to pack each purchase with love and care. Treat the package as if you were sending it to yourself. What would impress you as a shopper? Take time with the presentation because it is important. A shopper can receive your package and absolutely love their items but fail to shop with you again because of how you presented their purchase to them in your shipping. You want every shopper to become a loyal shopper. Let this reflect in the care you put into their package.

Tip: It is also a great idea to include a personal note thanking them for their purchase and offering them a discount off a future purchase. You can hand write these notes or you can have some professionally printed cards made as inserts for your shopper's packages. A great place to have package inserts made is www.VistaPrint.com. They always have a great sale going on. Just a small helpful tip!

STEP TEN

Believe in Yourself
Keys to Success

In order for any of these steps to work, you must apply the last step through this entire process. You must fervently believe in yourself and the E-Boutique business you are building.

Do not talk yourself out of your own success. We can be our own worst enemies. Starting any business is challenging. Being the boss is challenging. Alternatively, and thankfully, this will be one of the most rewarding tasks you will ever have accomplished. There will be times where being the boss can be so challenging that you reconsider why you started. This is perfectly normal. Keep in mind that only the strong survive and quitters do not succeed. Remember that anything worth having is working hard for. If one form or platform of marketing is not working for you, do not quit. Repurpose your efforts into what will work. Focus only on positivity and growth.

Made in the
USA
Columbia, SC